LEADERSHIP:
THE GOOD, THE BAD, AND THE UGLY

Peter Pollock

First Edition 2023

ISBN 9781088028421 (Paperback)

Mirage Publishing an imprint of The Paper House Books
Toms River, NJ 08753
www.thepaperhousebooks.com

Foreword

Every once in a while, you meet a person that becomes an immediate connection. While they are far and few in between, such people exist with the purpose of making a difference. These people tend to have three common traits that make them special: character, competence, and commitment. Upon first meeting Peter Pollock in Okinawa, Japan, all three of these traits were ingrained in his DNA, manifested via his passion for his people, the mission, and his military service. I immediately developed a professional relationship with Peter that is now a lifelong friendship based on respect, candor, and love for country.

His story is unique in many ways, from his Australian descent to his military service during the longest armed conflict in military history. I am glad he decided to pen down his humble beginnings because, over many chats and dinners having conversations, I always found out something new about Peter. From his witty personality to his passion for service and his lack of tolerance for mediocrity, he has never pulled any punches, always calling it as he saw it. A true sign of a man of conviction, he never caved into pressure and stayed true to his moral compass.

During his military service, I personally witnessed a man standing for the right and never siding with the compromising wrong. I witnessed a caring leader that had the utmost consideration for the well-being of his people, striking a fine balance between toughness and compassion. And I also saw a committed family man that was as true and consistent as the sun rising, symbolizing the beginning of a new day. Peter Pollock is indeed a good human being.

While our leadership philosophies have been extremely similar, there have been times of disagreement between us. But even during those times, one can see that the man lives a life of devotion to bettering mankind by owning the responsibility for his thoughts, actions, and outcomes. It was during those disagreements, which were not many, that I realized the value of his character and his commitment to doing good. Still, to this day and regardless of the topic, I can comfortably carry on with an hour-long conversation with him knowing that at the end, both of us will be better off for it. In a society that is quick to cancel, judge, and insult people with different opinions and stances, Peter serves as an example of unbiased regard for concern and progress.

Pay close attention to his lessons as he has poured his glass-encased heart into the following pages to help others be better. I have benefited from this over the past decade since I first met him, and now you too can be exposed to a good-natured human that cares about our society uniting once again to post 9/11 levels. I am fortunate to have such a leader to look up to and a friend to rely on in good times and bad times. Peter has never turned his back on me and if you were to meet him, he would have yours too. Peter, strength and honor my dear friend. And thank you for writing this book, and for allowing me the honor to be a part of it.

- Ramón "CZ" Colón-López, Senior Enlisted Advisor to the Chairman

"This book is a must for those leading in the hardest part of any organization - the muddy middle. The muddy middle leader must translate the guidance from above to accomplish the organization's mission while simultaneously translating what is actually happening on the ground to those above who can't see that ground clearly. Peter helps to show the way to be the leader who can do both. As a retired senior military leader, I had the privilege to work with Peter in peacetime and war. The lessons he shares come from the heart of a leader passionate for real people in the real world. Take the time to read this work, pass it around, and talk about it. You and your organization will be better for it."

- Jack L. Briggs, Major General, USAF (ret), Ed.D

I would like to thank the following people for their motivation, editing, and brutal honesty to help me get this book finished. Thanks to CZ, Carolyn, Regan, Jeff, Daniel, Jack, Brian, Tara, Mark, Richard, and Lisa. Most of all, I would like to thank my family. Thank you to Ako, Reina, and Emily, for your continued support and living this journey with me. I love you more than you know.

CONTENTS

Introduction

Leadership is hard. Leadership is important. And leadership means giving your time.

When I was a dumb, young captain teaching Air Force Reserve Officer Training (AFROTC) in 2001, something happened that changed my life. I had a cadet in his first year of college. He was a scholarship winner, super gifted athletically and academically, and he wanted to be a pilot in the Air Force. His path looked gold plated. One morning after PT, he approached.

"Hey sir, got a minute?"

I was sweaty; he was sweaty.

"Not right now," I said. "How about you come by my office this afternoon."

He never came by. He died during the night. I don't know what he wanted to talk to me about, but you better believe that I have never made the same mistake again.

If someone purposefully seeks you out, don't be selfish because you're afraid you might have to stay late or you feel you're too important. Don't search for a reason not to talk. Drop everything you are doing and make sure they are okay. Nine times out of ten, they are going to say, "Hey, let's play golf, grab lunch, have morning coffee," but the exception will be my cadet.

Trust me. You do not want the weight of my mistake on your conscience.

I have thought about this for a long time; maybe too long. The thought has been in my head for what seems like forever – not just any book, a book about leadership. But it's more than that. This is a book about a journey, the journey of my life. It's also about what leadership is, what leadership is not, and the pitfalls of leadership. Let's call it a memoir. It's based on a class I have been teaching for several years. Now is the time to put it on paper.

Let me tell you up front, this book will not be written with elegant language, superior prose, or $10 college words. Instead, this story about

1

a man and his journey in life will come at you written in a conversational tone. Hopefully, it's down to earth and will speak to you so you feel like, "Hey, this is something I can do; this is something anyone can do." Let's begin there.

So, who am I and what makes me worthy of writing a book like this? My story begins back in 1967 believe it or not. My father, a navigator in the Royal Australian Air Force, was chosen to transfer to Nellis Air Force Base in Nevada to train on the newly purchased F-111 aircraft. There were only 24 of them. Australia had purchased the package of aircraft from the U.S., and from what I have been told, my father was selected as the senior navigator. He was instructed to train on them and bring them back. Towards the end of the three years at Nellis, I came along. I was fortunate enough to be the recipient of dual citizenship by birth. Something destined to determine my future approximately two decades later.

My parents separated when I was eight, and as was done back in those days, my mum picked my brother and me up, put us in the back of an old Capri, and drove to old Studley Park Road in Kew, a suburb of what I consider my home, Melbourne (Victoria), Australia.

Mum enrolled us in private, Catholic all-boy schools trusting that we would excel and she would not have to worry about us. Problem was, I was a little brat as a kid. The class clown was suspended multiple times for fighting, being loud – basically for being a little shit. Didn't get the attention at home, so I acted up to be the center of attention everywhere else. And it worked, to my detriment.

I remember attending Burke Hall in, oh, I don't know, maybe sixth or seventh grade. I got the strap (a large leather belt-like object that the headmaster would hit your hands with, leaving bruises) and a steel ruler across the back of my legs (like right at the crease in the leg behind the knees) so many times that I still have marks to this day. Corporal punishment was meant to work; it didn't for me, I rebelled even more, resulting in more adverse punishment. Fun times, not really...but sure was an experience.

I would have said "a learning experience," but I can't tell you what I learned from it. I only earned the wrath of my mother every time she was called away from work to come and pick me up at the school, or from after school detention…yeah, fun times. The beginning of a long, arduous relationship struggle with my mother. That's not close to a "woe is me," just reality.

Fast forward to 1985. My mum said, "We're going to live in Hawai'i." I said, "Excuse me?"

"Yeah, we're going to see if you like the United States 'cause it's not looking good for you over here, and you have dual citizenship. It'll be a blast."

We arrived in Hawai'i after a long, long flight, settled into a condo apartment and got all registered for school. I attended Maryknoll High School for the second semester of my freshman year and the first semester of my sophomore year. Very bizarre timing considering the differing school years. Then, at the beginning of 1986, she said, "That's it, we're going back home." What the heck was going on? Whatever.

Perhaps a defining point in my life occurred in May 1986. There was a movie released, perhaps the greatest recruiting tool for the U.S Navy: Top Gun. Yea, I know you are rolling your eyes right now, like, can this be cornier or what? Well, to help you stay interested, I never flew, and I joined the Air Force! So yes, saw the movie. I was like, "My father flew, so it only makes sense that I fly." I wore glasses with the old coke bottle lenses. I knew I couldn't be Maverick (Tom Cruise), so I decided then and there I wanted to be Goose, the Radar Intercept Officer in the back. Surely I didn't need perfect eyesight to do that.

Well, turns out you need better eyesight than I had. Back to original plan of joining to Navy. I found a host family back in Hawai'i (happened to be the principal of Maryknoll who opened his home to me) and in August of 1987, I packed up my bags and left Australia, basically emigrating to the United States and taking advantage of that dual citizenship thing I had going on courtesy of my parents.

So, how the heck did I end up in the Air Force? I walked down to the Reserve Officer Training Corps (ROTC) area on the University of Hawai'i campus expecting to find Navy. You know, Pearl Harbor, the home of the Pacific Naval Fleet, a ton of history so on and so forth. Nope, nada, nothing. No Navy ROTC…unbelievable. Only Army and Air Force. I thought,

3

Well, my brother was in the Royal Australian Army, and I was not a bush kind of guy, so I'm not having any of that. Hey, maybe I can fly in the Air Force.

You can fly in the Army too, but it's not nearly as cool. My father retired from the Royal Australian Air Force, so I decided to give it a go...only made sense. The rest, as they say, is history.

I was commissioned in 1993, served for 24 years, had 12 assignments (location wise), three deployments, (two in combat areas), and retired in 2017. My leadership background involved (starting at the age of 25 as a first lieutenant) being placed in positions of increasing authority. These ran the gamut: element chief, section chief, flight commander, division chief/director, deputy squadron/group commander, and squadron commander. My last assignment was in command of the largest single squadron in the Air Force, approximately 2,400 personnel, which is where the next part of this story begins.

Why am I doing this? True story. I was sitting in my room in a hotel in Las Vegas when my phone rang. It was the current group commander at Kadena Air Base in Okinawa, Japan. She said, "Pete (I much prefer Peter), I need you to come over here and take over the 18th Force Support Squadron. They are broken, they have a culture problem, and I need your help in getting it right." Have to admit got a little bit excited at the opportunity.

My wife is from Okinawa. I knew she would absolutely be in heaven if I took an assignment back there, so I said yes, with enthusiasm. Six weeks later I was assuming command of the squadron. Sixty days into command, I gave a climate survey. A climate survey in the corporate world measures an organizations pulse. It was geared towards giving me an assessment of the current situation on the issues, good and bad, in the unit. The results were all over the place, overwhelmingly negative, but there was a singularly similar pattern throughout the survey: the first line leadership was horrendous, not good, out of whack. As all good commanders do, I called in my trusted senior enlisted advisors (my chief and my first sergeant), shared the results, and asked them straight up, "Any recommendations on how to approach fixing this problem?"

They said, "Sir, the answer is simple. If leadership, or lack thereof, is the problem, put together some talking points based on your leadership experience, what works, what doesn't work, and take it on the road."

So I did. I constructed a 45-minute class of how to (and how not to) be a leader. The first time I taught it was in a closed session with about 45 of the first line leaders named in the climate survey. Most of the initial class members were civilians with some junior NCOs (Non-Commissioned Officers, think first-time supervisors in the corporate world) mixed in. Word got out, and I ended up opening the class up to the entire base, teaching once a month, sometimes more frequently.

Who would have thought that a kid from Australia, moving to Hawai'i to pursue a dream, would be teaching leadership to the personnel of the largest overseas United States Air Force combat wing? I could not have imagined this scenario in my wildest dreams. This book is an extended version of my class.

I mentioned the leadership positions I held. We were trained in leadership at every stage of officer professional development, but one person had a major impact on me. He believed my style of leadership worked and could be taught.

Chief Master Sergeant Ramon Colon-Lopez served as the 18th Wing Command Chief (Kadena Air Base, Okinawa, Japan) while I was assigned there as the Deputy Commander, 18th Mission Support Group. "CZ" as he is affectionately known has a very simple approach to leadership. And I copied it. CZ says, "Tell them what they need to hear, not what they want to hear."

"Need" and "want" are two very different approaches. If you tell someone what they want to hear, and keep telling them what they want to hear, they will never learn, nor will they ever grow. They will keep believing what people tell them because of a lack of honest and candid feedback from subordinates, peers, and superiors. However, if you tell people what they need to hear, they will learn, they will grow, and paradoxically, they will trust you more than anyone else. Hence, you should tell them what the need to hear: good, bad, or ugly. Using that philosophy as a basis for this book, I have an uncanny skill of telling people what they need to hear, not what they want to hear, sometimes to the chagrin of the people closest to me.

5

As you go through the pages, I will talk about what leadership is, and what it is not. There is an adage in the military, and perhaps in other places also, but it goes something like this: "You learn your best leadership from your worst leaders." I disagree. What you learn from your worst leaders, and I have had a few, is what not to do. It is almost as important, if not more so, to understand how not to be a leader. Accordingly, I will cover how to be a leader, and how not to be a leader: what to avoid doing. I will also mix in military examples, of course, and corporate examples where appropriate. I will do a deep dive into specific, real-world instances I have observed in the corporate world that are in complete contradiction to how we lead in the military.

I want to give credit where credit is due. Some of the ideas here come from reading about leadership, some come from watching people at work, and some come from videos I have seen on the internet or podcasts I have heard. Most of what you will read is based on my experiences of living through and growing from leadership situations. I will attribute and recognize sources as needed.

Let's get on with it shall we. It starts with "why."

Chapter 1: Why

Everything starts with why. It sounds simple, and it is; it's also very true. As mentioned before, I was requested by name to take command of the single largest Air Force squadron at the time. On the way to the assignment, I had to stop by Pacific Air Force's (PACAF) Headquarters at Hickam AFB in Hawai'i. The Pacific Air Forces (PACAF) commanding general was the first four-star female general in charge of a Major Command (MAJCOM), think 60,000 Airmen. General Lori Robinson gave us a book on the first day, Start with Why by Simon Sinek. I had never heard of Simon before. When I read, I was like, "Wow, this dude is spot on and knows what he is talking about."

The premise of the leadership tool here is simple. It's easy to know what you do and how you do your job, but understanding why, you do what you do is key. This is part of instilling pride into your team. If it's obvious that you understand why you come to work every day, the sentiment will spread across the team. Let me use the following as an example.

I currently work at United Services Automobile Association, or, USAA. It's a fabulous company with an even better mission. USAA serves the military and their families. The company is built on outstanding customer service and continuously maintains one of the highest customer service ratings ever across the spectrum of equals. Members are loyal because they know that USAA will do whatever is necessary to ensure take care of its members. We have a program that is run by military veterans (such as me) who work at the company: Zero Day PT.

According to USAA official branding "The mission of VETNet's Zero Day PT event is to provide employees with an orientation into military culture. This event challenges you in experiencing a day-in-the-life of our membership. It's a unique event you won't find anywhere else in corporate America, and gives folks an opportunity for personal insight into the meaning of the phrase, 'We know what it means to serve.'" The busses roll up at zero dark thirty (quite early in laymen's terms) and before the new folks even get off the bus, cadre (former veterans with a dash of active-duty training instructors thrown in for good measure) are in the employees' faces. They really do try to replicate what every member that has served (we allow family members to join also) has experienced. After the employees (yes, they are regular employees of the company and most of them have no military background or connection at all) get off the bus, they are hounded by almost every one of the cadre members for the next four hours. At the end of the morning, employees are predominantly moved emotionally. The program is designed to give them an understanding of why they come to work each day. Bottom line: understand why you come to work each day and instill that in your employees. It's not an easy task, but it should be one of your priorities as a leader.

Once you understand why you come to work every day, we can begin the discussion about the difference in generations, the way they think, and your ability to understand this as a leader. When I was a junior captain, someone told me, "It's your job to adapt to your boss, not the other way around." While this may have been true 25 years ago, it is no longer accurate. While at the end of the day, the boss makes the decision and you must support them (this will be discussed in detail later in the book), they need to understand that they have to embrace, and sometime adapt to (or at the very least respect) the differences in generations. It's all cyclical in my opinion.

The youth of today are wearing similar stuff to what we wore in the 70s and 80s, but don't tell them. Let me impart a story to shed light on what I am talking about.

There I was, in the food court of the Base Exchange in Okinawa. I was eating lunch by myself across from two one-stripers (think 19 or 20 years of age), who had more than likely joined the military out of high school. They appeared to be maintainers (fixing aircraft for the most part) and friends. However, they did not even look at each other the entire lunch, let alone speak to each other. They ate their lunch. In between bites, they thumped away on their electronic devices. I am very aware of the plague of gun violence in this country, so I use this example with great caution. But my first thought was if an active shooter had come in, they would have taken selfies with the shooter in the background, posted it on social media, and then dropped to the ground and kept on texting. Probably not 100% accurate as to their reaction, but I'm trying to make a point. I could have chosen any scenario involving a melee; back in the 80s and 90s, I would like to believe that someone would have tried to intervene, to stop the ruckus. Today, it's easier to take your phone out, record what's happening, and post it on social media in the hopes it will go viral. Generations think and act differently.

I gave the following scenario to hundreds of folks during my time teaching. You're my boss and you have two employees: a 70s child (me) and my coworker who just graduated from college, first job. As our boss, you give us the same directions, the same instructions, using the same tone of voice, nothing different at all. Would we take that direction and process it differently? The answers I got were always a resounding yes, without a doubt.

This is not good. This is not bad. This is the way it is. Different generations have different skills, advantages, and abilities. They react and process ideas and directions differently. Today's generation grew up surrounded by data, information and capabilities we were not exposed to back in the 70s, the 80s, or even the 90s. The ability to access information has an upside and a downside for sure. Social media, IMHO, has many more negatives than positives. The access to and need for instant gratification/satisfaction has changed the way people think. The lesson: as the leader, you must understand the differences, respect the differences, and adapt. Also, develop the ability to recognize your top performers. They are not always the yes person (someone who always agrees). Adapt accordingly.

Let's move on.

Further stories from Simon's book, Start with Why, include one about Southwest Airlines. They were struggling in the latter part of last century (sounds like a long time ago right) and Herb Kelleher, co-founder, and former CEO, got all the employees in a room and asked them something along the lines of, "Who is the most important person to the success of this company?" Everyone said, "It's the customer, it's the person that flies with us, etc. etc." Herb said, "No, you're wrong. The most important person to the success of this company is you, the employee." The takeaway from this example is the employee should be more important to a company, not the customer. No matter what you think of Southwest, the premise remains true.

Here's the lesson: unless you, as a leader, take care of the employee first, they will have no desire to take care of the customer or return the favor to you. Studies show this. If you treat your employees like crap, they will in turn treat the customers like crap. Conversely, if you treat your employees well, and take care of them, consciously or unconsciously, they will take care of you, the company, and the customers. No less than two former CEOs of USAA said something along the lines of, "No member experience can or should be better than the best employee experience." They got it. Take care of your people folks.

It's simple; leadership is a privilege and a responsibility, which segues into something Jack Welch said, "When you were made a leader, you weren't given a crown, you were given a responsibility to bring out the best in others." That's really your main job as a leader. Yes, a rather simplistic view of leadership, but maybe it is that easy. Take care of your people, encourage, motivate, and enable them to complete their jobs and you will be ahead of the game.

Now folks, I'm not telling you to be weak, to give in to your folks' demands and wishes, and to become the yes person. In fact, be the leader who has high expectations. We will assume that the average person can meet basic standards such as arriving to work on time, not lying, etc. Set the bar high and hold people accountable, but apply performance standards consistently. Different levels of employees, depending on experience, probably should have a different bar. You can't expect a new college grad to meet the same performance standards as someone who has 20 years of experience. There is going to be a learning curve for sure. But set the bar and give your folks the tools and the training necessary to meet it. If they don't, hold them accountable. "Train, transfer, terminate" in that order. An old crusty retired Marine Command Sergeant Major told me that once. My reaction? "Damn, glad I didn't join the Marines!"

One more item to remember along this same idea is that sometimes a fit does not work…and that's okay. You must be able to recognize that. Sometimes the fit fails because of work ethic, laziness, lack of motivation, something not related someone's ability to perform. Leaders must recognize deficiencies. Likewise, great leaders realize that sometimes a fit may not work due to honest skillset mismatch. The person may possess the cognitive or physical abilities to meet the requirements of the position, and they can make a good employee. Then your job should be to assist them to the best of your ability and help them find a good fit − or get them the training required to perform appropriately. Find the reason, understand it, and fix it. Treat the root cause (for all you six sigma people). Don't work on the symptom.

Let's talk about the difference between confidence and arrogance. There is a thought pattern among some people in positions of leadership that, "I am better than fill in the blank." The reasons do not matter because the premise is not true. No one is better than anyone else. No one. You may be more skilled or educated. You may shoot better or run faster, but don't think for one second those skills make you a better person. Thinking of yourself as a superior human being, leads to arrogance. Arrogance has no place in leadership…none…period.

Confidence is different. Confidence is good to have and necessary in leadership. Confidence is smiling, knowing you are doing the right thing. Arrogance is looking down on people, thinking they are not as good as you.

Sure, you know some bad people. (So do I, and they will be named in the next book. That's a joke, relax). There are toxic human beings, murderers, rapists, career criminals. Yes, they are bad people, but leaders should never look down at someone, never think of themselves as inherently better. At the end of the day, we are all human.

11

There is also no place in leadership for braggarts. In the military, we used to call them "one uppers," "chest thumpers," "look at me." Imagine sitting around a table for staff meeting or having lunch and you're shooting the breeze with friends, coworkers, whoever. You had a good round of golf on the weekend and say, "Hey, I shot well on the weekend, shot a 95." There is always one person who says, "Well, I played on the weekend, and I shot a 91." Or you mention you went fishing on the weekend. "Hey, I caught a pretty nice fish on the weekend, a 10-pound trout." "Bob" has to pipe up, "Mine was 12 pounds." We all know people like this and we all feel sad for the person because: 1) they are irritating as sh*t; and 2) they are usually making up stories to look better, seem relevant, or validate that they belong.

I gave my class to a group. One of the team members stopped me right as I was talking about one-uppers and stated that she was a recovering one-upper. There was a golf clap from the rest of the team. The moment was light-hearted, it was real, and I gave her huge kudos for having the guts to come out and admit she was the one who liked to have a story that was just a little cooler than everyone else's. There is no place in leadership for these folks.

Going one step farther, Herb Kelleher, who I have mentioned before, said, "I forgive all personal weakness except egomania and pretension." I think the use of the word "pretension" is remarkably applicable to someone who is a one-upper. "Pretension" is defined as, "the use of affectation to impress." Boom. Enough said. Don't be that guy.

Let's look at a specific example of arrogance versus confidence. Leaders can be confident, in fact, they probably should be. Don't be arrogant. Arrogance involves looking down on someone, thinking you are better. There is no place for arrogance in leadership, but let's be honest, it exists everywhere. A person in one of my sessions stated that he unequivocally believed the culture of the United States breeds arrogance. I don't disagree. Believing you must be the best at everything is not a good way to think. Don't ever be arrogant and look down on someone. It is unbecoming as a human being.

12

The following occurred in November 2015. I was sitting in my office in Okinawa, Japan, on a Sunday morning. Two young ladies were about to fight each other in the octagon. One of them was an up and comer; the other, a tried-and-true champion – absolutely brilliant at her craft, and cocky, extremely arrogant. Well, ladies and gentlemen, what do you think happened? The champion, undefeated in the arena, verbalized her arrogance. When the challenger smiled and offered to tap gloves, the champion refused, her first mistake. She got destroyed, knocked out; it was one of the biggest upsets in history according to some. Colin Powell once talked about tying your ego to your position. In this case, he was right. She lost the crown. In fact, she never won again and slunk away into oblivion in the arena that had put her on such a pedestal, primarily, they loved her arrogance, but it proved to be her downfall indeed. The story highlights how arrogance will bring you down.

Confidence smiles; arrogance smirks.

Let's take a quick look at character and integrity and how they work together. One of the clearest and most common traits of being an effective leader is character. How is integrity connected with character? Integrity is the foundation of someone's character. A leader's character must be beyond reproach. Once you lose integrity, everything else you do is suspect. It's very difficult to regain solid ground. People begin to question everything you do. Can someone reestablish trust? Possible yes, but very difficult.

People often confuse leadership with a title. Funny, leadership has nothing to do with a title. I get some of my best quotes from LinkedIn and Facebook, or whatever it chooses to call itself now. One of the more "direct" quotations I found was attributed to Craig Groeschel: "We don't need a title to lead. We just need to care. People would rather follow a leader with a heart than a leader with a title." Another comment I found while trolling social media said, "Leadership is not a position on an org chart, it's an act." Both comments are accurate.

You also must care. You must give a damn. If people know you care about them as a person, care about their family, care about what sports team they follow, they will go beyond what is expected, because they know it's appreciated. If you are enamored with your title of "Director" or "Vice

President," people will not follow you and you will fail. Some of the best leaders are people without titles. Get to know them, do what they do. Care.

A Vice Wing Commander I used to work with during my first squadron command knew all the names of his folks' spouses, their kids, and their birthdays. Seemed robotic for sure, and takes an incredible memory, but his people loved that he gave a damn. He cared.

When you do have the honor of leading people, ask yourself, "How do I take care of them?" "Do they matter to me, or do I matter to them?" "How do I talk to them; how do I give them instructions, guidance, tasks?"

Everything we do as people, as human beings, as leaders, is received by others. How they receive it is just as important as how you deliver it. Consider the following. When talking with your team, do you use "I" more than "we"? "We" is inclusive, and talks about the group, or the team. "I" centers the attention on yourself. Leadership is not all about you. This is just one of the differences between being a "boss" and being a "leader."

Let's explore some other traits, or differences, between a boss and a leader. A boss usually takes credit for something as opposed to giving credit to the team. When your team has a success, don't take credit, give it to the members. Without the team, you are nothing.

Know the difference between micromanaging and delegating. Which do you do? Some folks are confused about what micromanaging is. When you closely watch, control, continuously provide input on how to do a task, yes, you got it, you are a micromanaging. This shows that there is no trust or freedom for your folks to think on their own. Not a good technique.

Leaders delegate and give their people the freedom to find out how to complete a task their own way. If you are going to sit there and tell me how to do a task you have assigned, then do the damn thing yourself. A boss critiques; a leader encourages.

We have all heard the glass half full/half empty comparison. A positive outlook versus a negative one. Colin Powell said that perpetual optimism is a force multiplier. The opposite is also true. Constantly being a half glass empty person is overwhelming and unpleasant. We all know that life is not full of rainbows and unicorns. Being a realist is valuable, but continually

14

beating your people down and finding what's wrong with their work or their attitudes is not conducive to positive leadership nor a positive work environment. Encourage your people and point out the good parts of what they do. Don't solely focus on weaknesses; focus on strengths also. If someone needs to improve in one area, instead of loathing the situation, do something about it. You are responsible for providing the tools and training to improve your folks. Focus on "can," not "cannot." Don't blame others; take responsibility. I will go into blame versus responsibility in the next section.

If your folks make a mistake, own them as the leader of the team. Coach more than you direct. People will accomplish, hear me, people will accomplish more if you coach and encourage instead of commanding or demanding actions from them. Shut up and listen...stop blabbering and listen. If you're talking more than your team, you're done. People don't want to listen to you dragging on about something, especially if it's about what you did as a leader. Who cares? Pay attention to your folks. Many of them will contribute immensely to the team.

Inspire enthusiasm, not fear. Being real is not the same as instilling fear. Know the difference. Scare tactics don't work, and if they do, it's for a short period of time. Coach and inspire, don't direct or use fear. Is there a time and a place or a "one-way conversation" as they call it in the military? Absolutely. But, this should be the exception, not the rule. If you find these one-way conversations happening all the time, one of you has an issue.

Remember what the old Marine said. Maybe it's a train, transfer, or terminate situation. Finally, and this comes with a caveat (and yes, most of my former military folks reading this are going to roll their eyes), don't command, ask. You can get people to accomplish so much more simply by stating "Do you mind," "Would you mind," "Can you take care of..." This is a different approach from, "You will do this," You get the picture? Now, let me tell you a story.

There was a leader who took my class and set up some time to talk to me afterwards. She told me of an employee who, no matter how or how many times she was asked to do something, did not respond to accomplishing a task. I told her, "Sometimes, you gotta 'go boss.'"

15

Sometimes you must have the one-way conversation. Sometimes, you are very direct. There are folks out there that only respond to direction… and stern direction at that but it is the exception, not the rule. I can count on one hand (okay, maybe two hands) the number of times during my 24-year career that I had to "go boss" and have a one-way conversation. It was usually ugly. And it usually only happened once. After that, you employ short-term memory and move on. Get over it; it's done; no grudges. Again, going boss can occur but it needs to be the exception not the norm.

Humility. I've spoken about this at length. In life, generally, we should be humble. But in leadership, humility is critical. In almost every level of Professional Military Education (PME), you see clips from old war movies, which have a lesson in leadership tied to them. In the book Killer Angels (and the movie by the same name), there is a scene between General Lee and General Stuart. Lee calls Stuart into his office. Stuart enters the room and snaps a sharp salute. Lee returns it. He tells Stuart that some other men claim Stuart is not cutting the mustard. Stuart's initial reaction is what probably most people would do; he bucks up and says, "Tell me who these men are," or something of that nature. Lee had given orders to Stuart to do recon on an enemy position and not to engage.

Stuart had ignored the orders and voluntarily engaged the enemy, so he's in a little bit of pickle. In those days, officers wore swords. Stuart offers his to Lee. The symbolism is clear. "If I no longer hold your trust, I resign my position." Instead of fighting and making excuses, Stuart realizes he made a grave error and is willing to step down.

Lee stops him, and, in a greater show of humility, puts the sword back in Stuart's sheath. He tells Stuart not to make the same mistake again and expresses his complete faith. Brilliant display of humility on both sides.

Humility is a necessary trait for great/effective leaders; it's not negotiable.

Chapter 2: Reset, Relieve, Renew

I sometimes wonder how people can be so incredibly callous, why they are just downright mean to others. The past 24/36-odd months have been downright crazy (for clarification purposes, I am penning this at the beginning of 2023, so coming out of or at least trying to extricate ourselves from the pandemic). One might say, as an entire planet, we may have even regressed. But remember I told you no one is better than anyone else? Well, that's because at the end of the day, we are all human.

When I was at Kadena, I hosted the PACAF (Pacific Air Forces) Commander. A four-star general. You know who I chose to escort him at the dining facility? Not the flight commander. Not the chief. Not the NCOIC. No, I chose the youngest ranking airman, the most junior person in the unit. You know why? Because at the end of the day, we are all basically the same. The fact that one was on top of an organizational chart and the other one was at the very bottom, didn't bother me in the slightest. Your position on an org chart should not matter; the way you act and carry yourself makes you a leader. Got it yet?

If you feel the need to tell someone how good you are, you're probably not very good. We could go down an entire rabbit hole on this topic alone, but simply put, you have insecurities about yourself if you keep one-upping everyone. Life is not a game; you don't have to win all the time. If you are a one-upper, you may find that your team will slowly morph and become a collection of one-uppers. It could go either way. They could either follow what you do because for some unimagable reason they think it's cool, but more likely, they will become less and less interested in sharing their stories with you and the rest of the team because they know you will always come up with a better one.

The next story is about every leader having a window and a mirror. This is not my illustration, though many have claimed it. Someone in one of my classes relayed it to me. If your team has a success, they meet a deadline, they crush a deliverable, they have some measure of success in a task, your job as a leader is to use that window to look outside at your team and give credit to them for making something happen. It is not the time to look at the mirror, gloat, and say "look at me, look at what I did," because the success does not belong to you. It belongs to your team. Look out the window to give credit.

On the flip side, if something goes wrong, your team misses a deadline, they make a mistake, they fail to produce an adequate deliverable, do not look out the window and find someone to blame. Instead, go look in the mirror. The person who owns the failure is looking right back at you. You are responsible for the failures of your team. You should be looking in the mirror and asking yourself what you could have given the team, what tools and training you could have provided, to ensure success. A strong leader accepts blame and gives credit; a weak leader gives blame and accepts credit.

Never forget that.

Have you ever had a bad day? Sure, it's natural; people have bad days all the time. It's okay to have a bad day, but never in front of your team. The first time I put this bullet point up in my class, I was quickly interrupted with a correction from a "people leader" (what the corporate world calls someone who is above someone else in an organizational chart) in my class. She proceeded to tell me that her people tell her it's okay to have a bad day. It demonstrates her humanity. "And we're all human right?"

"Yes," I told her, "valid point, but let me explain the difference between your thought pattern and mine." I later amended the line to say, "Being human is okay, but when that turns into toxicity and negativity and starts to spread (and it will), then it's time for you to leave and reset."

This is what I am talking about. Remember the glass half full person? Well, in the same vein, negative energy spreads just like perpetual optimism. When your bad day turns into negative toxicity, it's time for you to saddle up and get out of Dodge to reset.

I had a boss come into work once when he was as grumpy as all get out. I went up to him after 30 minutes of being there. I asked, "Hey, you good?"

"Yeah, I'm good," he replied, but in a tone that shouted, "Nope, I'm not good."

So, I asked him again. (It is often said that you have ask someone at least twice before they give you an honest answer.) He replied, "Well, I do have something going on at home." It was clearly affecting him.

I told him, "Hey, it's noticed by the whole team. We got this, why don't you go and take care of whatever it is you need to take care of."

So, he left, and came back the following day a new person, or should I say, back to the old person he was. I later found out that he went and played a round of golf, solo. That was how he reset. That was how he released tension. Find what works for you to reset or release tension/stress, and use it. It's okay. Recognize your need and use your release to make things better. You know why? A bad attitude is like a flat tire. You can't go anywhere until you change it.

Chapter 3: Traits of a Successful Leader

I searched the Google universe and found hundreds of different lists with thousands of different traits of what makes someone a good leader. So how could I narrow it down to just four...really Peter, just four? Yes really... more than four is hard to track and these four were common among all the lists. So, sit back and get ready. I am about to unlock the secrets to being an outstanding and effective leader, IMHO of course.

1) **You must be able to communicate.** I'm going out on a limb here: this is the most important one. During my class, when I get to this point in the presentation, I ask folks, "Am I an introvert or an extrovert?" By then, I have been yapping at them, bantering, joking for about 40 minutes. About 80% of the folks immediately come back and say, "Extrovert, without a doubt." About 20% of the folks, who may be a bit more in tune with what's been going on, will perhaps allude to the fact that I might be introverted and know how to act extroverted. I might be an ambivert (resting on the cusp of both extra and intro). The truth is, in a Myers Briggs test, and I have taken it more than once, I am consistently a 1-point extrovert. The range goes from 0-20 on each side, 20 being the super extrovert or the super introvert. Here's why I am not a classic extrovert. If I go to a party (and I rarely ever do) and I don't know a single person, I will not talk to a single person. I will grab my free food (always the best kind), stand in a corner, and observe. I love watching people. Here's the difference, and it involves the importance of communication in leadership.

If someone introduces themselves to me, or I am introduced to someone by a third party, I can have a conversation. I can more than likely make a connection. You must be able to communicate. Food for thought. I learned in one of my professional military education classes of a study conducted where a group of general officers in the Air Force were given the Myers Briggs array: a large majority of them came back as "I," that's right: Introvert. Let's wrap communication into us all being human and not being better that anyone else. Here's another story whose origins are murky. I had a friend named Jim. He was taking the last class for his MBA. Let's say it was International Economics. The class was super hard. Jim had been studying for days to prepare for the final. He arrived at the testing room with the rest of the cohort and on each desk was a single sheet of paper. Jim was irritated. "What is going on? I studied all this time for one sheet of paper?" The professor looked at everyone and said, "Begin." Everyone turned over the lonely sheet of paper. There was one question. "What is the name of the janitor?" Everyone failed because no one knew.

The professor addressed the class. "Folks, I have taught you everything I know about international economics; you folks will go out into the world and do very well, but this, and the name of the janitor, is about life." Everyone is important. Know the name of the janitor. I worked on the third floor of a building with 19,000 other employees. I knew the name of the janitor, not because I was special; I wasn't the only one who greeted him when I saw him. But Juan would absolutely light up like a Christmas tree whenever someone said hi to him or asked about his day. He didn't think he belonged there, talking to folks in collared shirts and khaki pants. But he did, and those who didn't think they were better than others understood. Everyone has their lot in life, and no is better than anyone else. Learn everyone's name. I'm beating this drum hard because it is an essential part of being an effective leader. I can take credit for the next saying; I came up with it. I was in my first squadron command at Lajes Field in the Azores (Portugal). They probably chose the smallest squadron in the entire Air Force because they figured even Pollock couldn't screw that up. I sure learned a ton about leadership there by listening. I decided, "You can be as dumb as a box of rocks, but as long as you can talk to people, you can get them to do anything." Some people might say that the art of leadership is getting people to do what they really don't want to do, but making them feel like they wanted to do it in the first place. Sounds like trickery to me…it's not, it's good old simple communication. I have a P.E degree from the University of Hawai'i. That's Physical Education, not Petroleum Engineering. I was never the book smartest person in the room; you shouldn't try to be. But I could talk to people. Have that skill. If you don't have it, develop it. Steve Jobs said that if you are at the end of the table (i.e., the leader in the room) and you find that you are the smartest person in the room, find another room. Steve also said "I don't hire smart people to tell them what to do. I hire smart people so they can tell me what to do." Learn how to communicate and communicate well.

Here's my final point on communication. Never send someone else to give an important message. If you must, choose wisely.

My time in Afghanistan in 2010 can be broken down into two parts. The first half of my tour, I worked for a great guy. We respected one another. The second half of the tour, I worked for a different fellow. He clearly did not like me and the feeling was mutual. We just did not click. I completed my tour in November of 2010 and was replaced by a young lady in the same career field. I had been home for less than 30 days when I received an email at work on the unclassified network. It was from the second guy.

He said, "Check your SIPR (a classified system separate from our normal work area, usually in a classified vault.) I immediately thought, This can't be good. I opened the email. It read, "Your replacement was sent home for a family medical emergency; would you be able to come back and finish the rest of her tour?" That was it; no further explanation. My return would have taken a waiver for "boots on the ground in country" (a fancy way to say I had not been away from the combat zone long enough to reset before returning). Well, because the message came from someone I didn't like, I immediately went to the decision-making authority and told her about the email – and the request. I wanted her to let him know I could not return because I wanted nothing to do with him. He was going to have to suck it up or get a short notice replacement. She supported me, and I never returned.

Fast forward six months. I was having a phone conversation with Jack Briggs, the greatest man and leader I have ever worked for. Jack was the wing commander at Bagram during my tour in Afghanistan, the second time I had worked for him. I had the utmost admiration for him as a leader and as a human being. We were shooting the breeze and I told him the story about being asked to return. I sneered a little and said something like, "The hide on that guy."

Jack looked me square in the eye and said, "Peter, I asked him to send that email. I wanted you back."

I lost it. I broke down. "Sir," I said, "if you had sent the email, I would have been on the next thing smoking." (The next available mode of transport.) I would have gotten the waiver and gone without question.

The lesson: deliver the message yourself or be damn sure you send it via the right person.

2) You must like people. Oh, hold on now, wait, what? I must like people? Yes indeed. You can't be that classic 20-point introvert and hope that no one disturbs you. As a leader, you must be willing to engage people, and you have to be okay with the interaction. Liking people is different from wanting to be liked. Leadership is not, and I repeat not a popularity contest. We are in the business of people and there is no question about that. You must be available and be willing to interact with your people. Let's look at the flip side. If you want to be liked, don't be a leader. Go sell ice cream. Of course, not everyone likes ice cream, but you get the point. You also must be okay with the fact that not everyone is going to like you. This can be because they generally don't like anyone, or they disagree with a decision you made. Maybe they just plain don't like you. And that's okay. Bottom line, you have to like people and you shouldn't be a leader because you want to be liked; doesn't work that way.

3) You must be a possibility thinker. A lot of leaders who can't think of anything else, say, "Just get to yes." That's the dumbest thing I have ever heard. There may not be any possible way, legally or illegally, to get to yes. Some people might cringe when I say this, but I much prefer hearing, "What's in the realm of the possible?" Much better, and much more attainable. Let's say you call me. I'm in customer service or in position to provide guidance to you on some area. You say, "Hey Peter, I would like to accomplish A, B, and C, and I need them all to be done by such and such a date." More of a directive than a request, right? Let's say my initial answer, the very first thing out of my mouth is ,"Nope." You will do one of three things: a) Hang up; b) Ask to speak to a supervisor; or c) Argue with me, which is going to result in both of us getting heated with nothing being accomplished. Either way, the first answer of no is going to shut you down, and more than likely, piss you off. Even if "no" is the correct answer, it should never ever be the first answer. Let's try another response. "You know what, I don't think we can accomplish all of those items, but I can certainly help you get the first two done and we can see how far we can get with the third one." Much different answer and much different approach. Look for a way to work it. It's good to be loyal to the corporation or the area you work in, but possibilities do in fact exist; find them and be willing to work with them. You will find people come to you more often. To quote Colin Powell again, "The moment people stop coming to you with their problems is the day you stop being a leader."

4) You must be willing to learn. My final station in the Air Force was as commander of the 18th Force Support Squadron. Force Support was a combination of the old services career field and the old mission support career field. In corporate terms, think of an HR (Human Resources) area combining with an organization in charge of all the facilities, like the cafeterias, the fitness centers, lodging, etc. Ninety percent of the squadron I commanded was classic services. The rest was mission support. Guess where old Peter grew up: the mission support career field. I knew absolutely nothing about how to run a services career field organization. What I was willing to do, though, was learn. Our job as leaders is not to be subject matter experts (SME) in every single area. As Steve Jobs said, that's why we hire smart people. Our job is to know a little about a lot. The SME's job is to know a lot about a little. They're experts. Don't confuse the two. The old saying is still true: "Know enough to be dangerous." Surround yourself with SMEs who can teach you. If you can speak to a subject at a high level, you will be fine. If you need ground level information, you have two choices: go back and learn it or bring a SME with you. I prefer the latter.

Here's a classic example of a great leader who was not very comfortable in an area, and how he approached learning and growing. I was deployed to a combat zone in 2010. I was a deputy group commander and had great respect for my boss. He was a great dude, uber smart, and very calm. Almost every single day before he went for a walk around the camp to see his folks in action, he would stop by my area and ask me to go on the walk with him. (It wasn't really an ask.) Every time! Finally, I built up the courage to ask, "Sir, why do you keep taking me on these walks, or meet and greets with you?" He did not hesitate. He said, "Peter, I am not very comfortable talking to people, and you do it well, so I bring you, and maybe I will get better at it one day." He got it. He knew where he had a weakness (they call that opportunity in the corporate world so as not to offend anyone), and he strived to improve. Good job, or Bravo Zulu as they say in the Navy.

Chapter 4: Traits of a Successful Follower

Now, let me talk to you about followership. I have some very distinct thoughts about this subject. You may think you have read about these four traits previously, and you would be right. I have talked about them specifically or touched on them at least. But understand this; without these four traits, you cannot be an effective leader. All great leaders have been great (at least effective) followers at some point in their careers.

1) **Ego management and humility.** You've heard me mention humility. Yes indeed, followers need to be humble as well. Let's use me as an example, or any other former senior officer who has retired from the military and come to work in a large corporation as what they call "individual contributors." We are in charge of only one thing; a computer. As a follower, you must be humble enough to come in and roll up your sleeves. Be the person that the boss goes to when they have a question, when they need a task to complete. Be a team player, not the "look at me" person. Don't tread on people to get higher in the chain or to get the boss's attention. As they say in the military, "Do your ***** job. " (I can neither confirm nor deny the existence of the actual word.) Relate your good performance as it relates to team goals, and please, please, please, do not concentrate on winning personal awards. Do your job and do it well, and rewards will come, whether they are in the nature of a raise, a promotion, or public recognition. Head down, tail up, and do you job.

2) **Honesty.** Here's a concept that should be obvious to everyone, but some people are confused. Here's the type of honesty I am talking about.

This happened with a former supervisor of mine. The situation may or may not have been dependent on the fact that I have more years of experience and leadership, so the straightforwardness of your honesty and the conversations with your boss may have to be tempered, but hopefully you get the point. I was having my third quarter feedback. At the conclusion of the session, my boss asked, "So Peter, do you have any feedback for me?" I told her no. I was already exhausted and just wanted to exit stage left. She said, "Peter, you have never not wanted to share some feedback with me. C'mon, what do you have?" I reluctantly said, "Okay, I do have one thing." She said, "Shoot, let's hear it." "Okay," I said. "Open your door." She looked at me with a blank stare and said, "Huh?" I said, "You come in here in the morning, go into your office, and close the door. No matter what you are doing, it's closed. You open it to go to lunch, the bathroom, and at the end of the day. Your team sits out here on the floor and you are sending a clear non-verbal message that you are unavailable to your team. Open your door."

The next day, she came in, walked into her office, and left the door open. It was refreshing. No joke, I even had colleagues come up to me and ask if she was okay. I had to chuckle. Teammates started going to her office and asking, "Hey, you got a minute?" Where have we heard that before? That's the honesty I am talking about. Go and be honest enough to give feedback to your boss. But let me also give you a warning. Do not expect them to change a behavior or modify something simply because you gave feedback. They don't have to change their behavior; it is completely within their right. You gave them honest feedback, and that was your part.

3) **Loyalty.** In the military, we call this "carrying the flag." Nothing is more disruptive to a unit, a team, or a larger organization than the infamous water cooler "meeting after the meeting" where everyone trashes whatever decision the boss made. The time to cuss and discuss the pros and cons of a decision is behind closed doors. Let's say I must make a decision. If it doesn't have to be made quickly, chances are I will call a staff meeting to listen to the details, the pros and cons, and get educated on choosing A, B, or C. I'll consider the potential outcomes, good and bad. We have the meeting and a great discussion, then I decide. Not everyone is

going to like or agree with my choice – and you don't have to – but don't you dare go and meet with your folks or your peers and start badmouthing the decision. It's time for you to support the course that has been selected, right, wrong, or indifferent. I must live with the decision; I will be held accountable, especially if I made the wrong choice. If it's a right decision, great. If it's the wrong one, we adjust fire (move one way or the other to be more accurate in the decision and the results) and we learn. As a follower, you must be loyal and carry the flag. Any other action is detrimental to the unit. Full stop.

I'll leave you with this. Loyalty is not blind. You don't have to be a "yes man." That's something very different. In my experience, yes men are detrimental to the unit also. It's good to have an opinion and different thoughts. Be loyal, but don't be a yes man simply because you think the boss wants you to agree with him. And if your boss wants you to agree all the time, guess what, find a new job.

4) Be good at what you do. Many folks miss this concept because they are too worried about whether the boss is noticing them, if the boss likes them, and so on and so forth. Do your job and be good at it. A story to illustrate this point. My family and I were staying at a hotel awaiting on-base housing during a PCS (Permanent Change of Station). We went down to the complimentary breakfast on a fine Sunday morning. There was a long line for the omelets and there was only one dude making them. He was running solo, but he was super happy. He catered to every single person that placed an order. He handled multiple orders at one time. Clearly, he had a flare for what he was doing; he was confident, he was happy, and more importantly, he was very, very good. After we sat down, my eldest daughter asked me, "Dad, why was he so happy?" Fair question, I thought. The answer was simple. He was clearly good at what he did, he was enthusiastic, and he was glass half full kind of person.

I believe Abraham Lincoln said it long before Martin Luther King. "Whatever you are, be a good one." This is clearly what he meant. The guy made omelets for a living. He obviously enjoyed it, and he was surely good at it. Do your job and do it well.

Here is the second part of this trait, and it happened to me and made me a better person and a better leader. First squadron command at Lajes Airfield, I gave a climate survey as is the norm, about 90 days into taking command. It came back with one glaring and oft-repeated comment. "Major Pollock plays favorites." I was befuddled because I knew I did not have favorites. Still, as my executive assistant pointed out, I asked the same people to take care of this project or that one. And you know why? Because they were good at their job; they did their job well. So, I had to address the issue. The worst thing you can do as a leader is ignore something and pretend it doesn't exist. I assembled everyone in a commander's call and let them know I had heard them, and there was no excuse, but I was going to clarify why there was a perception of my having favorites. I told them, "If I don't ask you over and over to do projects, it's because at some point in time, you have shown me little desire, or more aptly, the expertise or knowledge to complete something I need. Those of you who I keep asking over and over to do projects have demonstrated the ability to do work and are good at it."

I can't continue without stating what you're all thinking. There is a downside to this, a double-edged sword. What's the reward for good work? Unfortunately, in many cases, it's more work. That doesn't mean you should go out and purposefully not do work to the best of your ability in the hopes of avoiding more work. No, absolutely not. But if you continue to produce outstanding work, two things will happen: you will probably get more work, and you will more than likely be the first one to be considered for that promotion. Do your job and do it well.

Chapter 5: Six For Success

Let's consider six areas the corporate world handles differently from the military. In layman's terms, and based on my long and illustrious five-year career, and IMHO, the corporate world struggles mightily with them.

Trust vs. Performance

I mentioned Simon Sinek before. I love what Simon talks about. Have I seen all of Simon's videos? No. Have I read all of Simon's books? Again, no. But from what I have read and listened to, Simon is spot on. In one video, he talks about performance versus trust.

He has worked with the Navy SEALS. He asked them point blank how people were chosen to be on SEAL Team 6, basically, the best of the best. It is highly specialized, high functioning, and chosen for our nation's most important and critical missions. SEAL Team 6 carried out the raid where Bin Laden was killed.

Here's what they told him. They drew a graph with two axes, one horizontal, one vertical.

The vertical axis was labeled Performance. The horizontal axis said Trust. Performance was how they did in the arena, on the battlefield. Did they do their job well? Did they excel? Classic performance. The Trust measurement dealt with the home front. Could they be trusted with your wife...your money?

On a relative scale, a person in the highest, far-right highest corner – high trust and high performance – was obviously someone you wanted. There aren't many. They are the unicorns. They're like the kids in high school you wanted to hate because they were super smart and athletically gifted – but they were also your best friend. Someone who was the highest performer with low trust was toxic. The SEALs told Simon they would prefer a medium performer and high trust, even a lower performer and high trust.

We're talking about – perhaps – the highest functioning team on the planet and trust is more important than performance. Think about it.

In the corporate word, how do we measure people? We try to use both parameters, but when you don't live and work and breathe around people all day (like they do in the military), how much do you know about their trustworthiness? That's rhetorical. I firmly believe the corporate world puts an abnormal amount of value on performance and promote those who perform well with a disregard for whether that person can be trusted. People in the corporate world put an inordinate amount of value on titles, offices, and the number of people they oversee. In other words, as Simon points out in the video, business places a high value on performance measuring metrics while disregarding the most valued trait for high performing organizations, trust. Businesses have a million and one metrics to measure performance, but zero or negligible metrics to measure trust. And every team has that one dude who is exceptional at the job but can't be trusted.

Ask any team, "Who's the asshole?" and they will all point to the same person. The same is true when you ask the team who is the person they trust the most. They will point to one individual (obviously not the one they indicated after the first question).

Get the trusted person on your team. And do it now. You can teach skill, you can't "teach" trust. You either have it or you don't.

Decision Making

I volunteer at my current place of occupation to give a 30-minute presentation for incoming employees. Let's call it a military panel. The panel gets a chance to interact with new employees before they are released to their supervisor. The new teammates have a chance to ask questions of our background, what it was like to transition, and maybe even the one thing everyone should know about a veteran and their experience. I was in a panel with a rather senior tenured executive who happened to be a retired senior enlisted guy from the Air Force (we had worked together during our military careers, so we knew each other). One of the new employees asked a rather interesting question I had never heard before, and have never heard since. He asked, "What does the military do well that we at this company do not?"

Valid question. My counterpart on the panel put his hand up like a stop sign and said, "Pete, I got this." I thought, This should be interesting.

His answer was sort of like this. "I can put a 19-year-old on the side of a mountain in Afghanistan, he knows when to move, he knows when to shoot, he knows when to call in CAS (close air support), he knows when to run and when to face the enemy. He is constantly making decisions for himself and his team. Here, we suck at making decisions!"

My jaw dropped not because I agreed with him 100%. I was just floored that someone as high as him in the ranks of the company had the backbone to say that flat out. I almost started to clap. From my observation, in the corporate world, we tend to try and "sell" our decisions to everyone to make sure they are okay with them. We don't want to hurt or offend anyone. We "hyper collaborate," a phrase I heard just the other day, and it's totally accurate. Some retired senior military leaders have failed to transition successfully as leaders in the corporate world because civilians don't jump and salute smartly at everything you ask them to do or about every decision you make. Food for thought.

Let me illustrate the absurdity to which I was asked to go to ensure that a group of people were "okay" with a decision. You might think it's a one-of-a-kind take, but I assure you it is not. My friends have had similar experiences. I was in a meeting with a former supervisor and their boss, the VP of the unit, the commander of the unit for all intents and purposes. (He was a former Army scout, with street cred on the ground in Iraq). He made a decision, and said, "Right, this is what we're going to do." He asked that we let the AVPs (think: flight/squadron commanders) know and move out. The AVPs are one level below the leader of the organization. Alright, let's get to it. My boss asked me to stay on the call after the VP hung up. I was asked to create a slide that would sell the decision to the AVPs. I kid you not. Wait, what? Help me understand this. The leader of the unit had just made a decision on the direction we were headed and I was being asked to create a slide to sell the decision and make sure the direct reports to the leader were on board with the decision?

As respectfully as I could, I said, "You have to be kidding me."

How about, maybe, a slide saying this is the decision and here is the data we used to make it. After a lengthy discussion, the boss decided the slide would show the reasoning behind the decision and the direction we were headed, a compromise of sorts, but a far cry from the initial ask of, "Let's sell the decision to the direct reports." The military is not perfect, but the corporate culture of selling decisions baffles me to this day. I have come to understand and accept (however reluctantly that may be) the difference between saluting smartly and carrying out orders, and gaining buy-in from your "stakeholders" even if those stakeholders are your direct reports.

My brother gave me the best advice ever upon my commissioning into the Air Force. He said "Peter, whatever you do, if you have the chance to make a decision, make a decision. Your people will respect you if you show the fortitude to make a decision." He was right. Not every decision is going to be correct. We make decisions and press. If they are wrong, then recalibrate. If it's right, great. More often than not I have had to adjust direction or make a slight correction to the original decision whether small or large. It's unlikely you will make the absolute perfect decision with no adjustments. But if you take one thing from this spiel, it is, "Make a decision and press." You can adjust if you must.

Here's the obvious thing. If you work for a boss where you are afraid to make a decision for fear of their response, or their anger, or their chastisement, guess what? Time to look for something else. No leader worth their salt leads by fear and holds all the decision-making authority. You need to make friends with the dude I mentioned above who is not afraid to disagree with the higher ups. Fear is a terrible way to lead. It's almost impossible to survive; it's impossible to be happy in that environment. I have worked for "fear leaders" and it is no fun. Find a new boss. Remember, people don't usually leave organizations, they leave their bosses.

Time Management

Manage your time, know what your priorities are. Ensure you know what's important to you. Events, family time. Don't let unimportant events take over your calendar. Know the difference between what is important and what is urgent. An urgent matter cannot be delayed. It demands immediate action. But, thankfully, most of us do not encounter urgent matters every moment of every day.

Important tasks can be put to the side until there is sufficient time to do them. They are not mission impacting. For example, I often say that if I had 10 bucks for each inbox I saw with hundreds, thousands (yes, thousands) of unread emails, I would be a rather wealthy man. The largest number of unread emails anyone in my class ever admitted to was 3,500. That's not a typo, he showed it to me. Was that the norm? Absolutely not, but it shows how failing to manage your time and priorities can get you behind really quickly. Let's assume that up to 50% of these emails in his inbox were junk, stupid stuff some bot sent to his email. Forty percent of them were ones where he'd been cc'd for situational awareness. The last 10% (which was still north of 350 unread emails) were probably important. Of those, how many were from people asking for a minute of his time?

Here is the way I handled it. With an organization such as my last command, you can imagine how many emails I received. My family knew I would go into the office, or log on to my work email from home on Sunday. That was when I went through my inbox and sorted what was junk, what needed a response, what should be forwarded, etc. I could start Monday morning fresh. If I didn't get to it Sunday, chances are I began Monday behind the eight ball, which is never good for anyone. Once my calendar kicked into gear, I was behind for the entire week.

Find a time management method that works for you and stick to it. Managing your time will allow you to accomplish the more important items on your to do list. And never miss an email from someone asking for a moment of your time.

Leadership vs. Management

For the longest time, the world I now work in called their "people leader" training. "Manager Candidate School." Huh? Why would you call a three-day course created to prepare high performing people to be leaders a "management" course? Management and leadership are different. Do they work together? Yes. Are they the same? Absolutely not.

Management is directing, controlling, working off a checklist. You can be trained for a management position. Leadership is an art that must be honed throughout time and developed. You lead people; you manage things. Leadership involves influencing, motivating, enabling people to do great things. I would add that effective leaders usually have good management skills. The reverse is not always true.

You can be the best manager in the world and not be a good leader. Learn the difference; understand it. And whatever you do, don't call your leadership development program "manager candidate school."

Results vs. Relationships

I had the privilege of taking a few courses from a former Vietnam POW. Colonel Lee Ellis speaks about leadership, leadership with honor, with courage, and engagement with honor. He uses real examples. He's a gifted orator. People stop and listen. The most fascinating part of his class is the "Leadership DNA" tests he has developed and gives to his students. It has two parts. Before the class starts, Lee asks everyone to take the DNA test, but saves the results until the end. He then asks participants to write down the best leader they ever worked for. Alongside their name, he asks them to put down whether the leader was results oriented, relationship oriented, or balanced in their approach. Results are driving delivery of a product or an end goal. Relationship oriented leaders concentrate on how they interact with others. A balanced approach would be someone who uses both equally, driving relationships to get results. It is certainly a fantastic and proportional way to lead.

Here's what the results show. (Keep in mind, both the test and the question have been administered to thousands of people, so a pretty large sample size.) Twelve percent of participants stated their best leader ever was results oriented. Thirteen percent responded that their best leader was relationship oriented. The remaining 75% said their best leader had a balance of results and relationships.

Let's pivot and look at the results of the Leadership DNA test. Forty percent were results oriented, 40% were relationship oriented, 20% were balanced. Think of it as a seesaw. Only two of every 10 respondents were balanced, but eight of 10 said their best leader was balanced. There is a large mismatch in what most people appreciate in their leaders, and what exists.

We need to focus more on the development of the skill that keeps us out of balance. I know everyone is wondering about my results. Well, the name of this guide is The Good, the Bad, and the Ugly, right? I am not balanced. To my surprise, I tilt slightly on the see-saw towards being results oriented. I know, I know; you can take the shocked look off your face now. I try every day to make the seesaw level. If you know the area where you need improvement, work on it. There is no shame in working on a weakness.

Great leaders recognize where they are lacking and strive to get better. Weak leaders ignore these areas and think they are great anyway. They will one-up you in a heartbeat. Learn to recognize them. There is reason why the seesaw leans a little bit to the results side. If you think about it, what are you more responsible for when you are higher in an organization, when you are more senior? Results or relationships? The answer is results.

Consequently, leaders in senior level positions are more focused on results. Having said that, you can use relationships to achieve those results. Be the balanced leader – not one or the other.

Intoxication of Power

Please pay attention to the following lesson/story. If you associate your leadership with a title or an office or a position on an org chart, and gloat about it, you will fail. You will fall. And more than likely, you will suffer the fate General Colin Powell warned about. "Avoid having your ego so close to your position that when your position falls, your ego goes with it." In laymen's terms, you will suffer from intoxication of power. You will end up with blinders on and be unable to see anything outside your world. Nothing to the left, nothing to the right.

You will associate power with your position. Not good. You will fail, and even if you don't, people will lose all respect for you. I've seen this first-hand, and it happens more often than you think in the military, in corporate world, in everyday life. If you fall into this trap, you will need a true friend, someone who has your back no matter what to tell you what's going on. Even then, you might be so engulfed with yourself that you may not even care.

This is a recipe for disaster. You will do stuff that you would not normally do and think it's okay because you are at the top of the food chain and no one else will know. You will be blinded. When the realization hits (and it's usually after you have been removed from your position or busted for something you thought you could get away with because you thought you were untouchable), it's too late. You will have to start again from scratch.

Trust me, it will happen. But, on the positive side, if this does happen to you, and you do fall, guess what you do? You get up, dust yourself off, learn from it, and rebuild yourself. It can be done. The learning and the rebuilding will make you a better person and a better leader. Remember, leadership is an action, not a position on an org chart.

I've lived it.

Summary

Let's wrap this up and put a bow on it, shall we? During the pandemic, I gave this class virtually. My wife would occasionally listen in on it, I guess. We have been married for a long time, and she knows and has heard most of these stories, but she comes up to me after one of my classes and asks me, "What makes you a good leader?" I thought this was like a trick question, like when your wife comes up to you and asks, "Does this dress fit me right?" Um, guys, there is no correct answer to this question by the way, and I thought she was laying a trap.

But she wasn't; she genuinely wanted to know why leadership was so important to me and why I thought I was an effective leader. It was a brilliant question, one no one had ever asked me before. So, I gathered all my gusto and answered in this way. "You remember the story I told you about going to a party and what I would do if I didn't know anyone? Remember if someone came up to me and introduced themselves, I could have a conversation? Well, I not only could have engaged in a conversation with them, but I also could probably make a connection with the individual."

That was my answer. Making a personal connection with someone you lead is vital to the relationship side of leading. Connecting with people can set you apart, level you up, help you on the highway of leadership. Make a connection; it can be about anything: family, sports teams, favorite food, the color socks they prefer. Find something you have in common make a connection. The next time you see them, you will immediately have something to talk about. (I was kidding about the socks by the way).

Let's follow this train of thought. I gave the Four Lenses test, a personality temperament array, to my daughters. Lo and behold, they each have different primary and secondary temperaments. They thought I was like a psychologist. Spot on. As a leader, you almost are a psychologist in the way you must be able to understand people, adapt, talk differently, listen differently, basically understand human interaction and the human dynamics on your team. It was such a basic comment, but oh so accurate.

Leaders do not run an organization. They steer the boat − guide the direction. A "leader" is not a position either (see earlier rant about associating your being a leader with a position). Simon Sinek specifically states, "It is not about being in charge, but about taking care of people in your charge." I could have written this entire book in about half a page: take care of your people...done.

More importantly, being a leader does not require you have a title. Having a title does not make you a leader. The way you act and the way you carry yourself will determine whether you are really a leader, not a position on an org chart.

Followers, you can determine whether the boat goes forward or stops dead in the water. The leader steers it, but you make it go. Followers are the engine to the machine, and guess what? If you do not want the boat to move, you can grind it to a halt. The sooner leaders understand this concept, the better. Followership is also important to any good leader.

I'm going to wrap up this trip down leadership lane with two stories. One from me, and one borrowed. These are the two most powerful stories I tell when I present based on the straw poll I take always after each class.

The year was 2006. I was attending Intermediate Development Education at the Air Force Institute of Technology. (AFIT had no idea I majored in gym). This was my first look (consideration) for squadron command. Every officer, at least, all the ones I know, strives to achieve one goal: to be a squadron commander. I was fortunate to be chosen and matched for the summer of 2007 as a squadron commander. I was so excited that I ran up to the dean of students at AFIT, and said, "Ma'am, I'm so excited I was matched to a command. What do I have to change about me to be a great squadron commander?" She looked at me with disdain, and said, and I quote "Nothing."

"What? What do you mean nothing?"

She looked at me and continued. "Peter, you were and have been chosen for command based on what you have accomplished and who you are as a person. We don't choose you to be a squadron commander because we 'hope' you will be someone that you're not."

Be who you are. That was the message: don't change. If you try to be someone you are not, you will fail. People will see right through you, and when the real you is revealed, you will never recover. Be who you are. Simple. You can't change your core personality, and you shouldn't try. To all you naysayers out there who might be thinking, That's not correct, he's just wrong, I will admit that you may have to modify behavior. You probably need to adjust some behaviors; there is a place and time for everything.

For example, I grew up in Australia, and spent 24 years in the military, and as my wife will tell you, I have a potty mouth, quite a bad one too. I probably should have joined the Navy (the veterans reading this will get that reference). So, that was a behavior modification of time and place I had to make. But it didn't change who I was at the core. Be who you are.

A well respected senior enlisted leader who I worked with, and who retired as the Senior Enlisted Advisory to the Commander of European Command (EUCOM) stated in his retirement speech that, "I'm just a regular guy in a special position." His statement is a summation and great illustration of a Simon Sinek story with which I will end.

Simon tells the story of his friend, who was, let's say, a retired Secretary of Defense (SECDEF). He was on stage one day at a conference. He was drinking coffee out of a Styrofoam cup while giving a speech about whatever retired SECDEFs talk about. He told the audience that two years prior, he was on this same stage giving the same talk as the SECDEF. He'd flown in first class, been picked up by a limo at the airport, and checked in at a five-star hotel where someone took his bags up to his room. He was shuttled to the same venue, and when he arrived, he was given coffee in a ceramic mug. Gold rimmed, everything. It probably said SECDEF somewhere on it.

On this occasion, he'd flown coach, taken a taxi to some random hotel, checked himself in, taken another taxi to the venue, walked into the green room and asked the attendant where the coffee was. The attendant pointed to the table in the corner, and he went and poured coffee into the Styrofoam cup that he was holding.

The moral of the story is this: the ceramic mug went with the position, not the person. Long after he is gone, someone else will enjoy the bells and whistles of being treated first class as he was. Those frills are not designed for the person; they are designed for the position. The sooner we grasp the concept, the better, because at the end of the day, each one of us deserves a Styrofoam cup.

I leave you with this. Stay humble, take care of your people, communicate, make a connection, and recognize you are human just like everyone else.

I bid you good luck.

Strength and Honor.

CPSIA information can be obtained
at www.ICGtesting.com
Printed in the USA
BVHW051158270423
663151BV00017B/842